"Mastering Value Selling

"Mastering Value Selling

Unlocking Success in the Competitive Marketplace."

Dr Livingston Rathnaraj

Dr Livingston

CONTENTS

CONTENTS

My journey

In a world where sales professionals are constantly striving for an edge, where competition is fierce and customer demands are ever-evolving, the need for a new approach to selling has become imperative. My name is Dr. Livingston, and after spending 24 years working in various sales positions across different verticals, I have come to a profound realization: it's no longer enough for sales teams to merely sell products or services to their customers. They need to do more—they need to convince, persuade, and demonstrate value like never before.

As I reflect upon my journey, I am reminded of the countless interactions I've had with customers, the lessons I've learned, and the successes I've celebrated. It was during the pursuit of my doctorate that I felt compelled to share my experiences and insights with fellow sales professionals and entrepreneurs. I wanted to create a guide that would empower individuals to effectively manage their sales efforts and unlock unparalleled success in today's competitive marketplace.

And so, I embarked on the writing journey that has led us to this moment—the creation of "Mastering Value Selling: Unlocking Success in the Competitive Marketplace." This book is not just another sales manual; The book is narrated as the journey of a salesperson eager to embark on a transformative journey of value-selling training.

In this fast-paced and dynamic era, customers are more discerning than ever. They seek solutions that transcend mere product features and benefits. They crave value—an assurance that their investment will yield tangible results, solve their challenges, and enhance their lives or businesses. The ability to effectively communicate and demonstrate this value has become the true differentiator in sales.

Throughout the following chapters, we will delve into the core principles, strategies, and techniques that will enable you and your team to become true value sellers. We will explore the power of cultivating a customer-centric mindset, uncovering customer value through meticulous research, and creating compelling value propositions that resonate deeply with your target audience.

But it doesn't end there. We will also address the importance of mapping value to the customer's decision-making process, customizing solutions for maximum impact, and mastering the art of demonstrating value through irrefutable proof and evidence. We will delve into the realm of building long-term customer relationships, overcoming challenges and obstacles, and navigating the ever-evolving digital landscape.

The goal of this book is clear—to equip you with the knowledge, skills, and mindset needed to thrive in the world of value selling. By the time you reach the final page, you will possess the tools to engage customers, win their trust, and secure long-lasting partnerships based on mutual value and success.

Whether you are a seasoned sales professional, an aspiring entrepreneur, or someone seeking to elevate your selling game, "Mastering Value Selling" is your trusted companion. Together, let us embark on this transformative journey and unlock the secrets to success in the competitive marketplace.

Introduction

In the fast-paced world of sales, where competition is fierce and customers are discerning, the ability to stand out and achieve remarkable success is the ultimate goal for sales professionals and entrepreneurs. Welcome to "Mastering Value Selling: Unlocking Success in the Competitive Marketplace," a comprehensive guide that will empower you to navigate the dynamic landscape of sales and elevate your performance to unprecedented heights.

In this book, we will embark on a transformative journey together—one that will revolutionize your approach to selling and help you master the art of value selling. Gone are the days of traditional sales techniques that focus solely on pushing products or services. Instead, we will delve into a powerful methodology that goes beyond superficial features and benefits, and delves deep into the core of what truly matters to customers: value.

Value selling is about understanding the unique needs, challenges, and aspirations of your customers. It's about crafting compelling value propositions that resonate with them on a personal and emotional level. It's about connecting with your customers, building trust, and nurturing long-term relationships. And ultimately, it's about unlocking your true potential for success in the fiercely competitive marketplace.

Through the pages of this book, we will explore the fundamental principles and strategies of value selling. We will uncover the secrets of cultivating a customer-centric mindset, uncovering hidden value, and crafting persuasive value propositions that capture the hearts and minds of your prospects. We will journey through the intricacies of mapping value to the customer's decision-making process, demonstrating value through concrete proof and evidence, and building strong, enduring customer relationships.

But this book goes beyond theory—it is a practical guide that equips you with actionable steps, real-world examples, and invaluable insights gained from years of experience. Drawing upon the wisdom of industry experts and successful sales professionals, you will discover proven techniques and strategies that will set you apart from the competition and propel you towards unparalleled success.

Whether you are a seasoned sales professional looking to take your skills to the next level or an aspiring entrepreneur seeking to establish a strong foundation for your sales efforts, "Mastering Value Selling" is your indispensable companion. It will provide you with the tools, knowledge, and inspiration needed to navigate the challenging terrain of the competitive marketplace, deliver exceptional value to your customers, and achieve your goals.

Are you ready to unlock the secrets of value selling and embark on a transformative journey towards unparalleled success? Let us dive into the world of "Mastering Value Selling" and unlock the key to your sales triumph in the competitive marketplace.

Introduction to Value Selling

In the bustling city of Salesville, there lived a group of sales professionals who were constantly on the hunt for success. Among them was a young and ambitious salesperson named Renu. She had heard whispers of a powerful sales approach called value selling and was intrigued by its potential to unlock untold success in the competitive marketplace.

One sunny morning, Renu found herself attending a sales conference where a renowned sales guru, Professor Anderson, took the stage. With a twinkle in his eye and a wealth of knowledge, he began unraveling the concept of value selling to the eager audience.

Professor Anderson explained that value selling was not just about selling products or services; it was about understanding the deep-seated desires and challenges of customers. It involved crafting unique value propositions that resonated with customers on a personal level, addressing their pain points and offering tailored solutions.

Renu's eyes widened with excitement as she realized that value selling went beyond the traditional sales approaches she had been familiar with. She had always been taught to focus on product features and competitive pricing, but value selling encouraged a shift in perspective—a focus on the customer's needs and desired outcomes.

As Professor Anderson continued, he highlighted the importance of differentiating value selling from other sales approaches. While traditional sales tactics often relied on persuasion, discounts, or flashy marketing, value selling stood out by prioritizing the customer's goals and delivering measurable results. It placed the customer at the heart of the sales process, fostering trust, and building long-lasting relationships.

The professor then turned his attention to the current state of the marketplace, emphasizing the importance of value selling in today's hyper-competitive environment. He revealed that customers were no longer swayed by empty promises or generic sales pitches. They sought value—tangible benefits that addressed their specific pain points and offered a clear return on investment. In a world where choices were abundant, value selling was the key to standing out and capturing the attention of discerning customers.

Inspired by Professor Anderson's words, Renu eagerly absorbed the key principles and benefits of value selling. The professor explained that active listening and empathy were essential in understanding the customer's perspective. By truly listening, sales professionals could uncover the customer's unique challenges and aspirations, enabling them to tailor their offerings to deliver maximum value.

To bring the principles to life, Professor Anderson shared a simple example with the audience. He told a story of a salesperson named Mark who had struggled to sell a new software solution. Mark initially focused on the technical features of the software but found little success. However, when he shifted his approach to value selling, he began engaging with customers to understand their pain points. He discovered that many customers struggled with time-consuming manual processes. Armed with this insight, Mark repositioned the software as a time-saving tool that would streamline operations, boost productivity, and ultimately increase profitability. By highlighting the tangible value of the solution, Mark closed more deals and forged stronger relationships with his customers.

To solidify their understanding of value selling, Professor Anderson engaged the audience in an activity. He asked them to imagine a product or service they were familiar with and challenged them to create a value proposition that cantered on addressing their ideal customer's specific needs and aspirations. Through this exercise, the audience experienced first-hand the power of value selling in crafting compelling value propositions that resonate with customers.

As the chapter drew to a close, Renu felt a newfound sense of excitement and determination. She had discovered a transformative sales approach that went beyond the conventional, one that would allow her to truly make a difference in the lives of her customers. With a heart full of inspiration, Renu eagerly anticipated the next chapters of her journey—ones that would delve deeper into the principles, strategies, and practical application of value selling.

Little did she know that her understanding of value selling was just the beginning, and the path to mastering this approach would take her on an adventure filled with challenges, triumphs, and remarkable growth. Together with her fellow sales professionals, Renu was ready to unlock the secrets of value selling and pave her way to unparalleled success in the competitive marketplace.

Building a Value Mindset

Renu embarked on her journey to master value selling. As she delved deeper into the realm of value selling, she realized that developing a strong value mindset was the foundation for success. She would explore the key aspects of cultivating a customer-centric mindset, identifying and understanding customer needs, nurturing empathy and active listening skills, and embracing a solution-oriented approach.

Renu found herself attending a special workshop led by a wise mentor, Sales Coach Anderson. With years of experience under his belt, Anderson had seen first-hand how a value mindset could transform sales professionals into trusted advisors for their customers. Eager to learn, Renu listened attentively as Anderson shared his wisdom.

Anderson began by emphasizing the importance of a customer-centric mindset. He explained that successful sales professionals put the needs and desires of their customers at the forefront. They viewed every interaction as an opportunity to understand the customer on a deeper level, going beyond surface-level conversations and striving to create meaningful connections.

To illustrate the power of a customer-centric mindset, Anderson shared a heart-warming story. He spoke of a salesperson named Alex, who had always been driven by quotas and targets. Alex's approach was transactional, focusing on closing deals as quickly as possible. However, after attending a transformative training session, Alex realized the significance of shifting his mindset towards a customer-centric approach.

Armed with newfound knowledge, Alex set out to understand his customers on a deeper level. He engaged in meaningful conversations, asking open-ended questions and actively listening to their responses. Through this process, Alex discovered that his customers were not just seeking a product; they were yearning for solutions to their unique challenges.

The story resonated with Renu, inspiring her to prioritize understanding her customers' needs. She recognized that by empathizing with her customers' pain points, she could tailor her approach to deliver personalized solutions. With renewed determination, Renu embraced the power of empathy.

Sales Coach Anderson emphasized the importance of active listening as a crucial component of a value mindset. He shared a valuable exercise with the workshop attendees. In pairs, they practiced active listening skills, taking turns sharing personal stories while their partner listened attentively. Through this exercise, Renu experienced the transformative power of giving undivided attention, understanding how it fostered trust and deepened relationships.

Anderson continued, explaining that a solution-oriented approach was another essential aspect of a value mindset. He highlighted that customers sought not only someone who understood their challenges but also someone who could provide actionable solutions. Sales professionals with a value mindset approached every interaction with a problem-solving mindset, focused on delivering tangible value to their customers.

Renu's mind was buzzing with ideas and newfound insights as Anderson concluded the workshop. She realized that building a value mindset was not a one-time endeavor, but rather an ongoing journey of growth and self-improvement. Renu vowed to continuously cultivate her customer-centric mindset, honing her active listening skills, and embracing a solution-oriented approach.

As Renu closed her notebook, she couldn't help but feel a surge of excitement. Armed with the knowledge and guidance she had gained, she was ready to apply the principles of a value mindset in her sales endeavors. Little did she know that her commitment to building a value mindset would propel her further on the path to mastering value selling and unlocking unparalleled success in the competitive marketplace.

5

Uncovering Customer Value

Renu's journey to mastering value selling continued. She understood that unlocking the true potential of value selling required a deep understanding of customers and their unique needs. This chapter would explore the art of conducting comprehensive customer research, utilizing effective questioning techniques, identifying pain points and challenges, and uncovering hidden value opportunities.

One bright morning, Renu found herself attending a specialized training session led by a seasoned sales strategist named Coach Anderson. Coach Anderson was renowned for his ability to unearth valuable insights about customers and transform them into actionable sales strategies. Renu eagerly settled into her seat, ready to absorb his wisdom.

Coach Anderson began by emphasizing the importance of conducting comprehensive customer research. He shared a captivating story of a salesperson named Max, who was determined to understand his customers at a profound level. Max invested time in studying his customers' industries, trends, and challenges. He pored over market reports, industry publications, and attended relevant conferences to gather valuable insights.

Inspired by Max's dedication, Renu realized the significance of research in uncovering customer value. She understood that in order to provide tailored solutions, she needed to gain a deep understanding of her customers' pain points and aspirations.

Coach Anderson then introduced the art of effective questioning. He highlighted that asking the right questions could unearth valuable information and create meaningful connections with customers. To illustrate this, he shared a powerful example of a salesperson named Michael, who had a knack for asking thought-provoking questions.

Michael would initiate conversations with open-ended questions that encouraged customers to share their challenges and goals. By actively listening to their responses, Michael could gain a clear understanding of their pain points and aspirations. Through effective questioning, he discovered hidden opportunities for delivering value that went beyond the initial surface-level conversations.

As Renu listened intently to Coach Anderson's words, she realized the transformative power of asking the right questions. She understood that by delving deeper into customer conversations, she could uncover valuable insights that would guide her in offering solutions tailored to their specific needs.

Coach Anderson then shed light on the process of identifying pain points and challenges. He shared a story about a sales professional named Anderson who had a remarkable ability to empathize with her customers. Anderson would listen attentively, putting herself in their shoes and truly understanding the obstacles they faced.

Through empathetic conversations, Anderson could identify pain points that were hindering her customers' progress. She recognized that by addressing these pain points, she could provide real value and become a trusted advisor to her customers.

Renu felt a surge of inspiration as she recognized the importance of empathizing with customers and identifying their challenges. She realized that by becoming attuned to their needs, she could offer solutions that would alleviate their pain points and drive meaningful results.

Finally, Coach Anderson revealed the art of uncovering hidden value opportunities. He stressed that beyond the obvious pain points, there were often hidden opportunities for value creation. These opportunities could arise from understanding customers' long-term goals, anticipating future challenges, or even offering innovative solutions that customers had yet to consider.

To illustrate this, Coach Anderson shared the story of a salesperson named James. James excelled at identifying untapped value opportunities for his customers. He would conduct thorough research, leverage his industry knowledge, and engage in insightful conversations to uncover value propositions that went beyond what customers initially envisioned.

As Renu absorbed these valuable lessons, she realized the importance of digging deeper and uncovering hidden value opportunities. She understood that by providing innovative solutions and anticipating customers' future needs, she could set herself apart from the competition and truly master value selling.

With the knowledge she had gained from Coach Anderson's training session, Renu felt empowered to embark on her journey of uncovering customer value. She knew that by conducting comprehensive research, asking effective questions, identifying pain points, and uncovering hidden value opportunities, she would become a sales professional capable of delivering exceptional value to her customers.

As Renu closed her notebook, she couldn't help but feel a sense of excitement. Armed with these powerful insights, she was ready to apply her newfound knowledge in her sales endeavors, eager to unlock unparalleled success in the competitive marketplace through the art of uncovering customer value.

6

Creating and Communicating Value Propositions

In the city of Salesville, Renu's journey to mastering value selling continued with unwavering determination. She understood that the ability to craft compelling value propositions and effectively communicate them was crucial to winning over customers. This chapter would explore the art of creating value propositions, aligning value with customer goals and objectives, utilizing storytelling techniques to engage customers, and communicating value in a clear and concise manner.

One bright afternoon, Renu found herself attending a captivating workshop led by a renowned marketing expert named Professor Anderson. With his charismatic presence and wealth of knowledge, Professor Anderson had a unique way of teaching the art of creating and communicating value.

Professor Anderson began by emphasizing the importance of crafting compelling value propositions. He shared a story of a salesperson named Sophia, who possessed a remarkable talent for presenting value in a way that resonated deeply with her customers. Sophia understood that a value proposition was more than just a list of features; it was a persuasive narrative that showcased the unique benefits customers would gain by choosing her solution.

Inspired by Sophia's success, Renu realized that crafting compelling value propositions required a deep understanding of customer needs and aspirations. She understood that by aligning the value proposition with the customer's goals and objectives, she could create a compelling story that would capture their attention and drive them towards a purchase.

Professor Anderson then introduced the power of storytelling as a technique to engage customers. He shared a captivating example of a salesperson named David, who transformed his sales presentations into compelling stories that transported customers into a world where their challenges were resolved and their dreams were realized.

David would paint a vivid picture of the customer's current situation, highlighting the pain points and challenges they faced. He would then introduce his solution as the hero of the story, presenting how it would address those challenges and unlock a brighter future for the customer. Through storytelling, David created an emotional connection that resonated with customers on a deeper level.

As Renu listened attentively, she recognized the transformative power of storytelling. She realized that by engaging customers through narratives that evoked their emotions and aspirations, she could captivate their attention and make her value proposition memorable.

Professor Anderson then emphasized the importance of clear and concise communication when delivering value propositions. He shared a story about a salesperson named Alex, who had struggled to communicate the value of a complex software solution. Alex realized that customers needed simplicity and clarity to understand how the solution would benefit them.

Inspired by Alex's journey, Renu recognized the significance of communicating value in a way that was easily understood and compelling. She understood that jargon and technical terms often confused customers, but clear and concise language could illuminate the true value of her offerings.

As the workshop drew to a close, Professor Anderson challenged the attendees to put their newfound knowledge into practice. He divided them into small groups and tasked them with creating value propositions for different scenarios. Through this activity, Renu experienced first-hand the power of crafting compelling value propositions, aligning them with customer goals, and communicating them effectively.

As Renu reflected on the workshop, she couldn't help but feel a sense of excitement. Armed with the insights and techniques shared by Professor Anderson, she was ready to embark on the journey of creating and communicating value propositions that would captivate her customers' hearts and minds.

With her notebook filled with valuable knowledge, Renu envisioned a future where she would confidently present her value propositions, employing storytelling techniques to engage customers and communicating the value of her offerings in a clear and concise manner. Little did she know that this chapter would be a turning point in her journey towards mastering value selling and unlocking unparalleled success in the competitive marketplace.

Mapping Value to Customer's Decision-Making Process

As Renu continued her quest to master value selling in Salesville, she eagerly delved into the, "Mapping Value to Customer's Decision-Making Process." She understood that in order to effectively influence customers' purchasing decisions, she needed to align the value she offered with their decision-making journey. She would explore the art of understanding the customer's decision-making journey, aligning value with different stages of the buying process, mapping value to customer needs and priorities, and addressing objections and overcoming barriers.

One sunny morning, Renu found herself attending a seminar led by a renowned sales strategist named Coach Anderson. With his vast experience and keen insights, Coach Anderson was well-equipped to guide Renu on her journey of mapping value to the customer's decision-making process.

Coach Anderson began by emphasizing the importance of understanding the customer's decision-making journey. He shared a captivating story of a salesperson named Mark, who was determined to uncover the nuances of his customers' buying process. Mark realized that by understanding the stages through which customers progressed before making a purchase, he could strategically align his value propositions to resonate at each step.

Inspired by Mark's success, Renu realized that she needed to gain a deep understanding of her customers' decision-making journey. She understood that by mapping value to each stage of the buying process, she could guide her customers towards a positive purchasing decision.

Coach Anderson then introduced the concept of aligning value with different stages of the buying process. He emphasized that each stage presented unique challenges and priorities for the customer. By understanding these stages, sales professionals could tailor their value propositions to address specific customer needs and concerns.

To illustrate this, Coach Anderson shared a story about a salesperson named Rachel. Rachel recognized that during the initial awareness stage, customers were seeking information and solutions to their problems. She crafted value propositions that highlighted how her offerings addressed their pain points and provided a clear advantage over competitors.

As the customer progressed to the evaluation stage, Rachel adjusted her approach. She understood that customers were now comparing different options and seeking evidence of value. Rachel provided case studies, testimonials, and detailed comparisons to showcase the tangible benefits her solutions offered.

Finally, as customers reached the decision-making stage, Rachel focused on addressing objections and overcoming barriers. She anticipated common concerns and proactively provided answers, building trust and confidence in her offerings.

As Renu listened intently to Coach Anderson's teachings, she realized the significance of mapping value to different stages of the buying process. She understood that by aligning her value propositions with customer needs and priorities at each stage, she could guide her customers smoothly through the decision-making journey.

Coach Anderson then shed light on mapping value to customer needs and priorities. He shared a story about a salesperson named Lisa, who possessed a deep understanding of her customers' desires and pain points. Lisa identified their specific needs and priorities and crafted value propositions that directly addressed them.

To illustrate this, Coach Anderson shared an example of a customer who valued sustainability and eco-friendly solutions. Lisa tailored her value proposition to highlight how her offerings aligned with the customer's values, showcasing their positive environmental impact.

As Renu absorbed these valuable insights, she realized the importance of understanding customer needs and priorities. She understood that by mapping her value propositions to address these specific concerns, she could demonstrate the relevancy and impact of her solutions.

Finally, Coach Anderson emphasized the significance of addressing objections and overcoming barriers. He shared stories of sales professionals who had encountered resistance from customers but skilfully navigated through objections to secure successful sales.

Coach Anderson provided Renu with strategies and techniques to address objections proactively and turn them into opportunities for value communication. He emphasized the importance of active listening, empathy, and providing evidence-based responses to alleviate customer concerns.

As Renu reflected on Coach Anderson's teachings, she felt a renewed sense of confidence. Armed with the knowledge of mapping value to the customer's decision-making process, she envisioned a future where she could seamlessly guide her customers through each stage, aligning her value propositions with their needs, and skilfully addressing objections and barriers.

With her notebook filled with valuable insights, Renu embarked on the next phase of her journey, ready to apply her newfound knowledge and overcome any obstacles that stood in the way of unlocking unparalleled success in value selling in the competitive marketplace.

8

Customizing Solutions for Maximum Value

Renu continued her pursuit of mastering value selling. With unwavering determination, she delved into the "Customizing Solutions for Maximum Value." She understood that in order to truly unlock success in the competitive marketplace, she needed to tailor solutions to meet specific customer requirements. This chapter would explore the art of customizing solutions, leveraging product knowledge and expertise, identifying upselling and cross-selling opportunities, and highlighting the unique value of her offerings.

One day, Renu found herself attending a seminar hosted by a renowned sales trainer named Coach Anderson. With his wealth of experience and dynamic teaching style, Coach Anderson was well-known for his expertise in customizing solutions for maximum value.

Coach Anderson began by sharing a captivating story about a salesperson named Max. Max was known for his ability to understand the unique requirements of each customer and tailor his solutions accordingly. He believed that a one-size-fits-all approach would not suffice in today's competitive landscape.

Inspired by MAx's success, Renu realized the importance of customizing solutions to meet specific customer requirements. She understood that by taking the time to understand each customer's needs, pain points, and goals, she could deliver a solution that truly addressed their challenges and added maximum value.

Coach Anderson emphasized the significance of leveraging product knowledge and expertise in the customization process. He shared stories of sales professionals who took the time to thoroughly understand their products, inside and out. By doing so, they were able to identify the unique features and capabilities that would align with the customer's requirements.

To illustrate this, Coach Anderson shared an example of a sales-person named Jason, who possessed extensive knowledge about his company's software solution. When he engaged with a customer, Jason showcased how the various functionalities of the software could be tailored to the customer's specific needs, providing maximum value and efficiency.

As Renu listened attentively, she realized the power of product knowledge in customizing solutions. She understood that by being well-versed in her offerings, she could identify the right components, features, or configurations that would create a perfect fit for each customer.

Coach Anderson then introduced the concept of identifying upselling and cross-selling opportunities. He explained that by understanding the customer's requirements, sales professionals could identify additional products or services that would enhance the value provided.

He shared a story about a salesperson named Alex, who had successfully identified an upselling opportunity when engaging with a customer. Alex recognized that by offering an upgraded version of the product, the customer would gain additional features and capabilities that perfectly aligned with their evolving needs. Through effective communication and showcasing the added value, Alex successfully upsold the customer, creating a win-win situation.

As Renu absorbed these insights, she recognized the importance of identifying upselling and cross-selling opportunities. She understood that by continually evaluating the customer's needs and staying informed about new offerings, she could uncover opportunities to provide even greater value to her customers.

Lastly, Coach Anderson emphasized the significance of highlighting the unique value of her offerings. He shared stories of sales professionals who effectively communicated the competitive advantages and differentiation of their solutions. By showcasing the unique features, benefits, and outcomes that set their offerings apart from the competition, they created a compelling case for customers to choose them.

Coach Anderson shared an example of a salesperson named Mia, who excelled at highlighting the unique value of her company's consulting services. Mia emphasized how their team's expertise, customized methodologies, and track record of success would result in transformative outcomes for the customer. Through compelling storytelling and tangible examples, she instilled confidence in the customer, illustrating the unique value they would gain.

As Renu reflected on Coach Anderson's teachings, she felt a surge of excitement. She realized that by customizing solutions, leveraging product knowledge, identifying upselling opportunities, and highlighting the unique value of her offerings, she could create a truly remarkable customer experience.

With her notebook brimming with valuable insights, Renu envisioned a future where she would expertly tailor solutions, provide exceptional value, and establish herself as a trusted advisor in the competitive marketplace. Little did she know that this chapter would be another stepping stone on her journey towards mastering value selling and achieving unparalleled success in Salesville.

9

Demonstrating Value through Proof and Evidence

Renu's journey to mastering value selling continued with unwavering determination. As she delved into the, "Demonstrating Value through Proof and Evidence," she knew she was about to uncover the secrets of showcasing value to her customers. This chapter would explore the art of providing testimonials, case studies, and success stories, utilizing data and analytics to showcase value, conducting product demonstrations and trials, and engaging in value-based negotiation and pricing strategies.

One sunny morning, Renu found herself attending a workshop led by a renowned sales expert named Coach Anderson. With his wealth of knowledge and captivating storytelling abilities, Coach Anderson was renowned for his expertise in demonstrating value through proof and evidence.

Coach Anderson began by sharing a captivating story about a salesperson named Michael. Michael was known for his ability to provide concrete proof and evidence of the value his offerings could deliver. He understood that customers needed assurance that the solutions they were considering would deliver the promised benefits.

Inspired by Michael's success, Renu realized the importance of providing testimonials, case studies, and success stories to showcase value. She understood that by sharing real-life examples of how her offerings had positively impacted other customers, she could instil confidence in her prospects.

Coach Anderson emphasized the power of testimonials in building trust and credibility. He shared stories of sales professionals who had collected testimonials from satisfied customers and used them as powerful selling tools. These testimonials highlighted the tangible results achieved and the positive experiences customers had with the solutions.

To illustrate this, Coach Anderson shared an example of a sales-person named Alex, who had successfully leveraged testimonials in her sales presentations. Alex would read out statements from satisfied customers, emphasizing the specific benefits and outcomes they had experienced. The impact was undeniable, as prospects could relate to the real-world success stories shared.

As Renu listened intently, she realized the power of testimonials in demonstrating value. She understood that by providing social proof, she could alleviate doubts and show her prospects that her offerings had a track record of delivering exceptional results.

Coach Anderson then introduced the concept of utilizing data and analytics to showcase value. He explained that numbers and statistics could provide solid evidence of the value offered by a product or service. He shared stories of sales professionals who had used data to highlight cost savings, increased efficiency, or improved performance achieved through their offerings.

To illustrate this, Coach Anderson shared an example of a salesperson named John. John presented data-backed case studies that showcased the quantifiable benefits his solutions had delivered. By presenting before-and-after scenarios and utilizing charts and graphs, he provided a visual representation of the value his offerings could bring to the table.

As Renu absorbed these insights, she recognized the power of data in demonstrating value. She understood that by presenting objective evidence, she could appeal to the logical side of her prospects and strengthen their confidence in the value she offered.

Coach Anderson then delved into the importance of conducting product demonstrations and trials. He explained that allowing prospects to experience the solution first-hand could be a powerful way to showcase its value. He shared stories of sales professionals who had conducted engaging product demonstrations, showcasing the key features and benefits that resonated with the prospects' needs.

To illustrate this, Coach Anderson shared an example of a salesperson named Lisa, who conducted interactive product demonstrations that immersed the prospects in the solution's capabilities. By highlighting the unique selling points and addressing specific pain points during the demonstration, Lisa effectively communicated the value that her offerings could provide.

As Renu reflected on these stories, she understood the significance of engaging prospects through product demonstrations and trials. She realized that by allowing them to see the value in action, she could create a memorable and persuasive experience that would stay with them.

Lastly, Coach Anderson emphasized the importance of engaging in value-based negotiation and pricing strategies. He explained that in value selling, it was crucial to align the price with the value delivered. He shared stories of sales professionals who had successfully negotiated based on the value their offerings provided, rather than engaging in price-focused discussions.

To illustrate this, Coach Anderson shared an example of a salesperson named Mark, who had effectively positioned his offering as a premium solution with exceptional value. Mark focused on highlighting the return on investment, long-term benefits, and the competitive advantage his offerings would provide. By emphasizing the value, Mark was able to negotiate pricing discussions based on the impact his solutions would have on the customer's business.

As Renu absorbed these insights, she recognized the importance of adopting a value-based negotiation approach. She understood that by anchoring the discussions on value and the tangible benefits her offerings brought, she could shift the focus away from price and negotiate from a position of strength.

With her notebook filled with valuable insights, Renu envisioned a future where she would skilfully provide testimonials, leverage data and analytics, conduct engaging product demonstrations, and negotiate based on the value her offerings delivered. Little did she know that this chapter would equip her with the necessary tools to convincingly demonstrate value to her customers in Salesville.

Building Long-Term Customer Relationships

As Renu's journey in mastering value selling progressed, she eagerly delved into the eighth chapter of her book, titled "Building Long-Term Customer Relationships." She understood that in the competitive marketplace, fostering strong and lasting connections with customers was vital. This chapter would explore the art of fostering trust and credibility, nurturing post-sale relationships for repeat business, leveraging customer feedback for continuous improvement, and harnessing technology to enhance the customer experience.

One sunny afternoon, Renu attended a seminar hosted by a renowned customer relationship expert named Coach Anderson. With his wealth of experience and warm, engaging presence, Coach Anderson was known for his expertise in building long-term customer relationships.

Coach Anderson began by sharing a heartfelt story about a salesperson named Rebecca. Rebecca believed that building trust and credibility was the foundation of any successful long-term customer relationship. She understood that customers needed to feel confident and assured that their best interests were at the forefront.

Inspired by Rebecca's approach, Renu realized the importance of fostering trust and credibility with her customers. She understood that trust was earned through transparency, honesty, and consistently delivering on promises. By consistently acting with integrity and demonstrating genuine care for her customers' success, Renu knew she could build strong, enduring relationships.

Coach Anderson then emphasized the significance of nurturing post-sale relationships for repeat business. He shared stories of sales professionals who went the extra mile to stay engaged with their customers even after the initial sale. These professionals understood that maintaining regular communication, providing ongoing support, and seeking opportunities for upselling or cross-selling were key to securing repeat business.

To illustrate this, Coach Anderson shared an example of a salesperson named James, who had built a loyal customer base by staying connected with them. James consistently reached out to his customers, providing valuable insights, updates, and personalized recommendations that aligned with their evolving needs. By nurturing these post-sale relationships, James ensured a strong foundation for repeat business and ongoing success.

As Renu listened intently, she recognized the importance of nurturing post-sale relationships. She understood that by going above and beyond, offering continuous support, and proactively addressing their needs, she could foster loyalty and create a customer base that would return to her for their future needs.

Coach Anderson then introduced the concept of leveraging customer feedback for continuous improvement. He explained that feedback from customers was a valuable source of insights that could drive innovation and improvement in products, services, and overall customer experience. He shared stories of sales professionals who actively sought feedback, whether through surveys, follow-up calls, or open dialogues.

To illustrate this, Coach Anderson shared an example of a salesperson named Megan, who regularly reached out to her customers to gather feedback. Megan genuinely listened to their concerns, suggestions, and compliments, using this feedback to refine her offerings and enhance the customer experience. Through this continuous improvement approach, Megan demonstrated her commitment to delivering value and exceeding customer expectations.

As Renu absorbed these insights, she realized the importance of actively seeking customer feedback. She understood that by valuing their opinions, addressing their concerns, and implementing necessary changes, she could build stronger relationships and ensure her offerings remained relevant and valuable.

Coach Anderson concluded the seminar by discussing the role of technology in enhancing the customer experience. He shared stories of sales professionals who leveraged technology to streamline processes, personalize interactions, and provide a seamless customer journey. Whether it was through automated follow-ups, personalized marketing campaigns, or self-service portals, technology played a crucial role in delivering a superior customer experience.

To illustrate this, Coach Anderson shared an example of a salesperson named Anderson, who harnessed technology to create a delightful customer journey. Anderson utilized a customer relationship management (CRM) system to track customer interactions, tailor her communications, and provide a personalized experience. This empowered Anderson to anticipate customer needs, proactively address concerns, and deliver a seamless and memorable experience.

As Renu reflected on these stories, she recognized the importance of leveraging technology to enhance the customer experience. She understood that by embracing digital tools and platforms, she could streamline processes, personalize interactions, and provide her customers with an exceptional journey from start to finish.

With her notebook filled with valuable insights, Renu envisioned a future where she would foster trust and credibility, nurture post-sale relationships, leverage customer feedback, and harness technology to create remarkable customer experiences. Little did she know that this chapter would equip her with the essential strategies to build strong, long-lasting customer relationships in the competitive marketplace of Salesville.

Overcoming Challenges and Obstacles

As Renu continued her journey toward mastering value selling, she eagerly delved into the ninth chapter of her book, titled "Overcoming Challenges and Obstacles." She understood that in the competitive marketplace, obstacles and challenges were bound to arise. This chapter would explore the art of dealing with price objections and competitive pressure, handling difficult customers and objections, managing sales team challenges and resistance to change, and adapting to market trends and disruptions.

One cloudy morning, Renu attended a seminar led by a seasoned sales leader named Coach Anderson. With his wealth of experience and a resilient spirit, Coach Anderson was known for his expertise in overcoming challenges and turning obstacles into opportunities.

Coach Anderson began by sharing a story about a salesperson named Alex. Alex faced a daunting challenge when a prospective client raised concerns about the price of his offering compared to the competition. Alex recognized that price objections were a common hurdle in sales and that overcoming them required a strategic approach.

Inspired by Alex's determination, Renu realized the importance of dealing with price objections and competitive pressure. She understood that it was crucial to communicate the unique value her offerings provided, focusing on the return on investment, long-term benefits, and the competitive advantage they offered. By highlighting the value proposition and demonstrating how it outweighed the price difference, Renu knew she could effectively address price objections.

Coach Anderson then shared stories of sales professionals who had encountered difficult customers and objections. He emphasized the importance of active listening, empathy, and reframing objections as opportunities for deeper understanding. These professionals understood that by addressing concerns head-on, offering alternative solutions, or providing additional evidence of value, they could navigate through objections and win over even the most challenging customers.

To illustrate this, Coach Anderson shared an example of a salesperson named Laura, who encountered a highly sceptical customer. Instead of becoming defensive or disheartened, Laura actively listened to the customer's concerns, acknowledged their perspective, and provided tailored solutions that directly addressed their needs. Through her patience, understanding, and commitment to delivering value, Laura successfully converted the sceptical customer into a loyal advocate.

As Renu absorbed these insights, she recognized the importance of handling difficult customers and objections with grace and perseverance. She understood that by genuinely listening, empathizing, and offering tailored solutions, she could turn challenging situations into opportunities for building stronger customer relationships.

Coach Anderson then shifted the focus to managing sales team challenges and resistance to change. He explained that change was inevitable in the dynamic business landscape, and sales teams needed to adapt to stay ahead. He shared stories of sales leaders who faced resistance from their teams when implementing new strategies, processes, or technologies.

To illustrate this, Coach Anderson shared an example of a sales leader named Chris, who encountered resistance when introducing a new CRM system to his team. Instead of forcing the change upon them, Chris engaged his team in open discussions, listened to their concerns, and provided training and support to ensure a smooth transition. Through his effective leadership, Chris fostered buy-in from his team, and they embraced the new system, realizing the value it brought to their sales process.

As Renu reflected on these stories, she understood the importance of managing sales team challenges and resistance to change. She recognized that effective communication, transparent leadership, and providing the necessary resources and support were key in navigating through such obstacles.

Lastly, Coach Anderson emphasized the significance of adapting to market trends and disruptions. He explained that the business landscape was ever-evolving, and successful sales professionals were those who embraced change and proactively adapted to new market dynamics.

He shared stories of sales professionals who were agile and quick to identify emerging trends, adjust their strategies, and leverage new opportunities. These professionals understood that by staying informed, continuously learning, and embracing innovation, they could stay ahead of the competition and thrive in a dynamic marketplace.

To illustrate this, Coach Anderson shared an example of a salesperson named Mike, who successfully adapted his approach to leverage emerging digital platforms and online sales channels. By recognizing the shifting preferences of customers and aligning his strategies with digital trends, Mike gained a competitive edge and expanded his customer base significantly.

As Renu listened attentively, she recognized the importance of adapting to market trends and disruptions. She understood that staying informed, continuously learning, and embracing innovation were essential in navigating the ever-changing business landscape.

With her notebook filled with valuable insights, Renu envisioned a future where she would confidently overcome challenges, handle objections with finesse, lead her sales team through change, and adapt to market trends and disruptions. Little did she know that this chapter would equip her with the necessary strategies to thrive amidst obstacles in the competitive marketplace of Salesville.

12

Mastering Value Selling in the Digital Age

As Renu reached almost the final chapter of her book, titled "Mastering Value Selling in the Digital Age," she was filled with anticipation. She understood that in today's fast-paced and technology-driven world, embracing digital tools and strategies was crucial for success in value selling. This chapter would explore harnessing the power of technology, leveraging social media and digital platforms, utilizing AI and automation, and embracing continuous learning to adapt to digital transformation.

One evening, Renu attended a conference led by a renowned digital sales expert named Coach Anderson. With his expertise in leveraging technology for sales success, Coach Anderson was a respected figure in the digital sales realm.

Coach Anderson began by sharing a story about a salesperson named Lisa, who recognized the transformative power of technology in value selling. Lisa understood that technology could streamline processes, enhance customer engagement, and provide valuable insights for sales professionals.

Inspired by Lisa's journey, Renu realized the significance of harnessing the power of technology in value selling. She understood that by leveraging digital tools and platforms, she could reach a wider audience, engage with customers on a deeper level, and streamline her sales process for maximum efficiency.

Coach Anderson then focused on the role of social media and digital platforms in customer engagement. He emphasized that in the digital age, customers were active on various social media platforms, seeking information, recommendations, and connections. He shared stories of sales professionals who effectively utilized social media to build their personal brand, engage with prospects, and share valuable content that demonstrated their expertise and the value they could provide.

To illustrate this, Coach Anderson shared an example of a salesperson named Anderson, who leveraged LinkedIn to connect with industry professionals, share insightful articles, and engage in meaningful conversations. Through her active presence on social media, Anderson not only built a strong network but also positioned herself as a trusted resource and thought leader in her field.

As Renu absorbed these insights, she recognized the importance of leveraging social media and digital platforms for customer engagement. She understood that by creating a compelling online presence, sharing valuable content, and actively engaging with prospects and customers, she could establish meaningful connections and demonstrate the value she could bring to their businesses.

Coach Anderson then introduced the concept of utilizing artificial intelligence (AI) and automation in the value-selling process. He explained that AI could analyse vast amounts of data, provide valuable insights, and streamline repetitive tasks, allowing sales professionals to focus on building relationships and delivering value. He shared stories of sales teams that implemented AI-powered chatbots, personalized recommendations, and data-driven analytics to enhance the value-selling experience.

To illustrate this, Coach Anderson shared an example of a sales team that utilized an AI-powered chatbot to provide instant support, answer customer inquiries, and deliver personalized recommendations based on the customer's unique needs. The chatbot not only saved time but also ensured consistent and accurate responses, enhancing the overall customer experience.

As Renu listened attentively, she realized the immense potential of AI and automation in value selling. She understood that by incorporating these technologies into her sales process, she could gain valuable insights, automate routine tasks, and deliver a more personalized and efficient experience to her customers.

Coach Anderson concluded the conference by emphasizing the importance of continuous learning and adapting to digital transformation. He explained that the digital landscape was constantly evolving, and sales professionals needed to stay abreast of the latest trends, tools, and strategies to remain competitive.

He shared stories of sales professionals who embraced continuous learning, attended industry conferences and webinars, participated in online courses, and sought mentorship to stay ahead in the digital age. These professionals recognized that by investing in their own growth and adaptation, they could navigate the digital transformation with confidence and success.

As Renu reflected on these stories, she understood the significance of continuous learning and adaptation in the digital age. She recognized that by staying curious, seeking new knowledge, and embracing change, she could become a master of value selling in the digital landscape.

With her book nearing completion, Renu felt a sense of fulfilment. She had embarked on a journey to share her experiences and insights in value selling, and now she had a comprehensive guide that would equip sales professionals with the necessary tools, strategies, and mindset to succeed in the competitive marketplace of the digital age.

Little did she know that her book, "Mastering Value Selling: Unlocking Success in the Competitive Marketplace," would inspire countless individuals to embrace value selling, harness technology, and thrive in the ever-evolving world of sales.

13

Sustaining Success through Value Selling

As Renu approached the final chapter of her book, titled "Sustaining Success through Value Selling," she felt a mix of emotions. This chapter would serve as the culmination of her journey, a reflection on the key principles and strategies she had shared throughout the book. It would reinforce the importance of value selling in a changing market, provide guidance for ongoing development and improvement, and inspire sales professionals to embrace value selling as a long-term strategy.

Renu sat down at her desk, ready to write the conclusion that would leave a lasting impact on her readers. She decided to approach it as a heartfelt story, one that would resonate with sales professionals on a personal level.

In her story, Renu introduced a character named Mark, a young and ambitious salesperson who had just finished reading her book, "Mastering Value Selling: Unlocking Success in the Competitive Marketplace." Mark was inspired by the stories, examples, and insights shared throughout the chapters. He had gained a deep understanding of the concept of value selling, and he felt empowered to apply it in his own sales career.

Mark embarked on his journey armed with the knowledge and principles he had learned. He embraced a customer-centric mindset, actively listened to his customers, and crafted compelling value propositions that aligned with their goals and objectives. He diligently mapped value to their decision-making process, customized solutions to their specific needs, and provided proof and evidence to demonstrate the value of his offerings.

Through the challenges and obstacles he encountered, Mark remained resilient. He overcame objections, handled difficult customers with grace, and inspired his sales team to embrace the value-selling approach. He adapted to market trends, leveraged technology to enhance the customer experience, and constantly sought opportunities for growth and improvement.

As Mark's story unfolded, Renu recapitulated the key principles and strategies introduced in each chapter of her book. She highlighted the importance of understanding the concept of value selling, differentiating it from other sales approaches, and recognizing its significance in today's competitive market. She reinforced the key principles of value selling, such as customer-centricity, empathy, active listening, and solution-oriented thinking.

Renu also emphasized the benefits of value selling, such as building trust and credibility, fostering long-term customer relationships, and driving business growth. She provided practical guidance for ongoing development and improvement, encouraging sales professionals to continuously refine their skills, embrace new technologies, and stay updated with market trends.

As Renu concluded her story, she inspired sales professionals to view value selling as more than just a sales technique—it was a mindset, a philosophy, and a long-term strategy for sustained success. She encouraged them to adopt a growth mindset, be open to learning and adaptation, and always strive to deliver exceptional value to their customers.

With her final words penned, Renu felt a sense of accomplishment. She had successfully shared her knowledge, experiences, and passion for value selling with sales professionals around the world. She knew that her book would serve as a guide, empowering readers to unlock their full potential and achieve remarkable success in the ever-evolving landscape of sales.

And so, as Renu closed her book, she smiled, knowing that the journey of mastering value selling had only just begun for those who dared to embrace it. The competitive marketplace awaited, and with the principles and strategies outlined in her book, sales professionals were ready to sustain success and thrive through the power of value selling.

14

Conclusion

As Renu reflected on her journey of writing "Mastering Value Selling: Unlocking Success in the Competitive Marketplace," she realized the profound impact it had on her own understanding of value selling. But more importantly, she recognized the potential it held for sales professionals who would embark on the same journey of discovery.

The overall learning from her was clear: Value selling is not just a sales technique; it is a mindset, a philosophy, and a strategic approach to building meaningful customer relationships and driving business success. Through the stories, examples, and insights shared in each chapter, Renu had conveyed the essence of value selling and its transformative power.

The outcomes of embracing value selling were vast and far-reaching. Sales professionals would develop a customer-centric mindset, understanding that their ultimate goal was not just to sell a product or service, but to provide exceptional value to their customers. They would learn to identify and understand customer needs, cultivating empathy and active listening skills to build trust and credibility.

By embracing a solution-oriented approach, sales professionals would go beyond simply highlighting product features or benefits. They would craft compelling value propositions that resonated with their customers' goals and objectives, effectively communicating the unique value their offerings could deliver.

Through comprehensive customer research, effective questioning techniques, and the identification of pain points and challenges, sales professionals would uncover hidden value opportunities. They would map value to the customer's decision-making process, addressing objections and overcoming barriers along the way.

The journey of value selling would also empower sales professionals to customize solutions for maximum value. By tailoring offerings to meet specific customer requirements, leveraging product knowledge and expertise, and identifying upselling and cross-selling opportunities, they would truly demonstrate the unique value their offerings brought to the table.

Furthermore, sales professionals would learn to demonstrate value through proof and evidence. By providing testimonials, case studies, and success stories, utilizing data and analytics to showcase value, conducting product demonstrations and trials, and engaging in value-based negotiation and pricing strategies, they would solidify their position as trusted advisors and solution providers.

Building long-term customer relationships would become a priority, as sales professionals fostered trust and credibility, nurtured post-sale relationships for repeat business, leveraged customer feedback for continuous improvement, and embraced technology to enhance the customer experience.

As sales professionals encountered challenges and obstacles, they would learn to overcome price objections and competitive pressure, handle difficult customers and objections with finesse, manage sales team challenges and resistance to change, and adapt to market trends and disruptions.

The digital age would present new opportunities, and sales professionals would harness the power of technology in value selling. They would leverage social media and digital platforms for customer engagement, use AI and automation to enhance the value-selling process and embrace continuous learning and adaptation to navigate digital transformation.

Ultimately, the journey of value selling would lead to sustained success. Sales professionals would understand the importance of continuous development and improvement, reinforcing their commitment to value selling as a long-term strategy. They would inspire others in their field to embrace value selling, setting the stage for a new era of customer-centric, value-driven sales practices.

As Renu felt a sense of fulfilment and excitement. She knew that the knowledge and insights she had shared would empower sales professionals to unlock their full potential, transform their sales approach, and achieve remarkable success in the competitive marketplace.

The journey of mastering value selling had only just begun for those who dared to embrace it. With each chapter, each story, and each lesson, sales professionals would embark on a path of continuous growth, delivering exceptional value to their customers and unlocking their own potential as true masters of value selling.